What Is COVID-19?

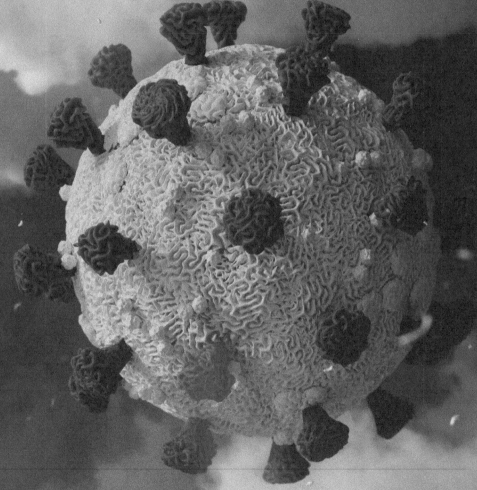

Alexis Roumanis

 Explore other books at:
WWW.ENGAGEBOOKS.COM

VANCOUVER, B.C.

ℯ WWW.ENGAGEBOOKS.COM

What Is COVID-19? Level 2
Roumanis, Alexis 1982 –
Text © 2020 Engage Books
Design © 2020 Engage Books

Edited by Jared Siemens
Cover design by: A.R. Roumanis

Text set in Arial Regular.
Chapter headings set in Arial Black.

FIRST EDITION / FIRST PRINTING

LIBRARY AND ARCHIVES CANADA CATALOGUING IN PUBLICATION

Title: What is COVID-19? Level 2 reader / Alexis Roumanis.

Names: Roumanis, Alexis, author.

Identifiers: Canadiana (print) 20200226754 | Canadiana (ebook) 20200226762
ISBN 978-1-77437-292-0 (hardcover). –
ISBN 978-1-77437-293-7 (softcover). –
ISBN 978-1-77437-294-4 (pdf). –
ISBN 978-1-77437-295-1 (epub). –
ISBN 978-1-77437-296-8 (kindle)

Subjects:
LCSH: COVID-19 (Disease)—Juvenile literature.
LCSH: LCSH: COVID-19 (Disease)—Prevention—Juvenile literature.
LCSH: Coronavirus infections—Juvenile literature.

Classification: LCC RA644.C68 R682 2020 | DDC J614.5/92—DC23

Contents

4   What Is a Virus?

6   What Are Coronaviruses?

8   What Is COVID-19?

10 How Does COVID-19 Spread?

12 How to Stop the Spread of COVID-19

14 Risks for Different People

16 How Does COVID-19 Affect Children?

18 What Is Social Distancing?

20 Social Distancing in Action

22 Why Is Social Distancing Important?

24 What Is a Vaccine?

26 How Technology Is Helping

28 Activity - How to Wash Your Hands

30 Quiz

What Is a Virus?

A virus is a very tiny germ. Germs can make people feel sick.

Viruses can survive inside life forms. People, animals, and plants are life forms.

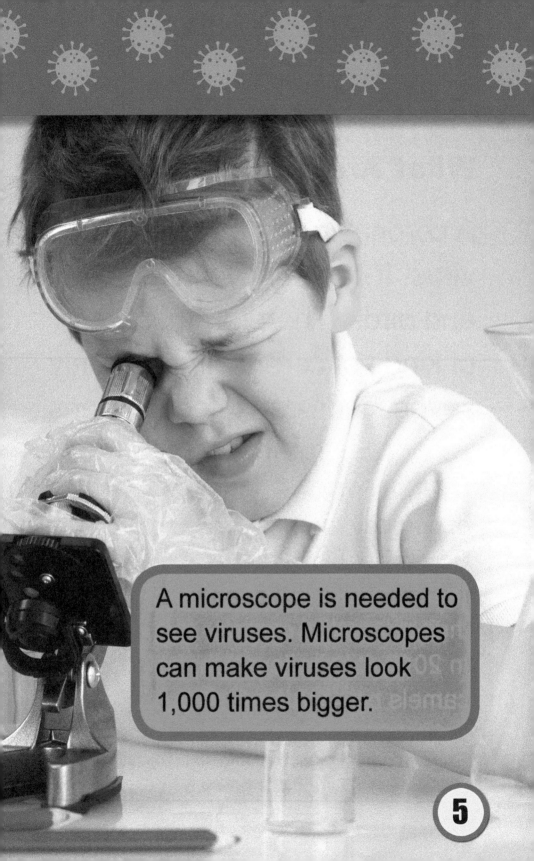

A microscope is needed to see viruses. Microscopes can make viruses look 1,000 times bigger.

What Are Coronaviruses?

A coronavirus is a type of virus. It can survive in mammals and birds. There are hundreds of kinds of coronaviruses. Only seven kinds can infect humans.

MERS is a type of coronavirus. Scientists think that it originated in bats, and then passed to camels. In 2012, it is believed that camels passed the virus to humans.

Coronaviruses are common.
They can make people feel
sick. Coronaviruses can
cause a runny
nose, a sore
throat, and
a cough.

What Is COVID-19?

COVID-19 is a new kind of coronavirus. It can spread easily between humans. COVID-19 spread quickly across the world.

Scientists think COVID-19 began in bats. It was first found in humans in Wuhan, China.

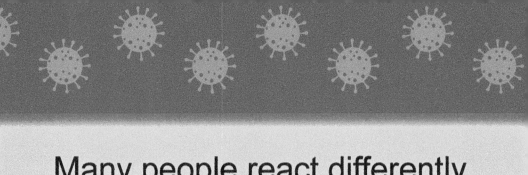

Many people react differently to COVID-19. Some people feel normal or slightly sick. Other people may cough, or feel warm. Usually they will find it difficult to breathe.

Only 1 out of 20 people with COVID-19 need to go to a hospital.

9

How Does COVID-19 Spread?

People can catch COVID-19 from tiny droplets. Droplets land on people when sick people sneeze or cough. COVID-19 can also live on things that people touch. Touching these things can make others sick.

Face masks can help stop the spread of COVID-19.

COVID-19 can survive in the air for up to three hours. The virus can survive on various surfaces for different lengths of time.

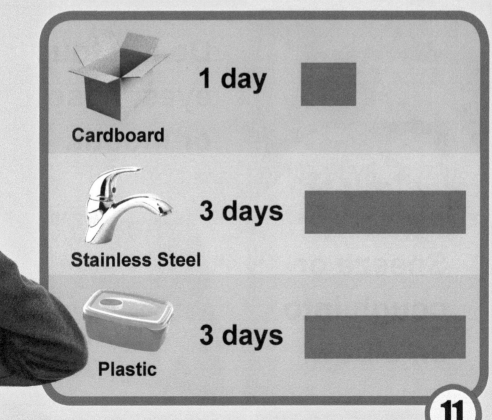

Cardboard — 1 day

Stainless Steel — 3 days

Plastic — 3 days

How to Stop the Spread of COVID-19

Wash hands with soap and water.

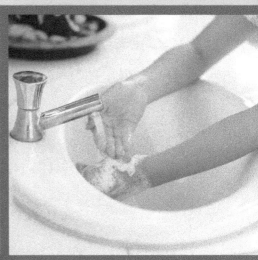

Do not touch eyes, nose, or mouth.

Sneeze or cough into an elbow.

(12)

Clean things that people often touch.

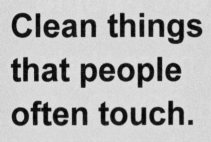

Do not share food and drinks.

Keep 6 feet (2 meters) away from other people.

13

Risks for Different People

Some people are more likely to become sick from COVID-19. Older adults struggle to fight off viruses. People over the age of 60 are at a higher risk.

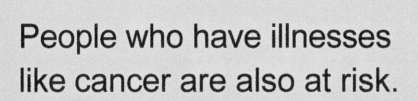

People who have illnesses like cancer are also at risk. Heart, blood, and lung diseases put people at high risk.

Healthy people are helping those at risk. Delivering groceries is one way they can help.

How Does COVID-19 Affect Children?

COVID-19 has little to no effect on young children. Children can carry the virus, though. They can pass it on to others.

In some places, COVID-19 spread quickly among adults. In these places, children played with their friends. Keeping away from friends is a way to slow the spread of COVID-19.

Children get sick from viruses quite often. They can catch about 6 to 8 viruses each year.

17

What Is Social Distancing?

Social distancing is a way to stop COVID-19. People social distance by staying 6 feet (2 meters) away from each other. It is meant for people who do not live together.

Keeping away from others makes it difficult for COVID-19 to spread. It is one of the best ways to slow the spread of an illness.

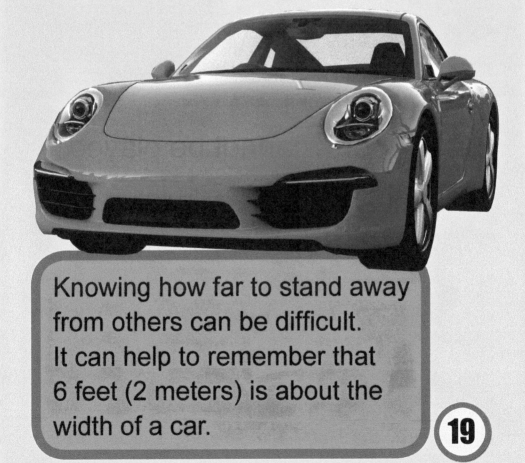

Knowing how far to stand away from others can be difficult. It can help to remember that 6 feet (2 meters) is about the width of a car.

19

Social Distancing in Action

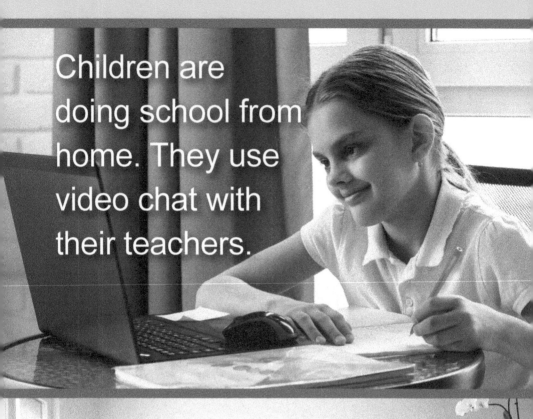

Children are doing school from home. They use video chat with their teachers.

Team sports cannot be played. Many people are exercising on their own.

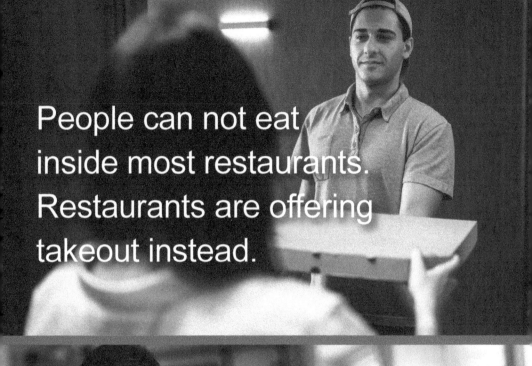

People can not eat inside most restaurants. Restaurants are offering takeout instead.

Many parents can not go to work. They are working at home using a computer.

Why Is Social Distancing Important?

Social distancing stops COVID-19 from spreading too quickly. If too many people get sick at once, hospitals may find it difficult to help everyone.

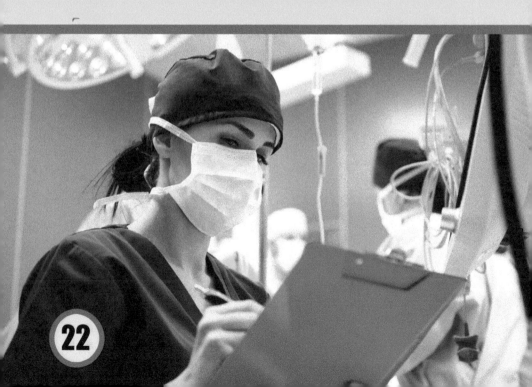

Social distancing helps make sure hospitals have enough breathing masks. These are needed to help people who can not breathe on their own.

What Is a Vaccine?

A vaccine is a type of medicine. It can help fight viruses. Vaccines teach the body how to fight a virus on its own.

COVID-19 could return every flu season. A vaccine can help to stop this from happening.

Many scientists think that a vaccine for COVID-19 could be made in about 18 months.

How Technology Is Helping

Breathing masks can be made with 3D printers.

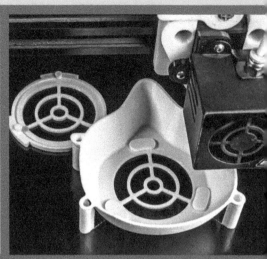

Car makers are building breathing masks instead of cars.

Drones can deliver things to people's homes.

Robots can kill COVID-19 with invisible beams of light.

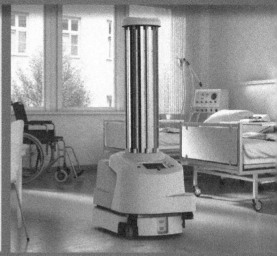

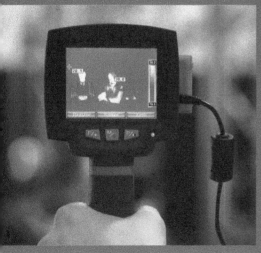

Special cameras can check if people have high body temperatures.

Automatic soap pumps stop germ spread in public washrooms.

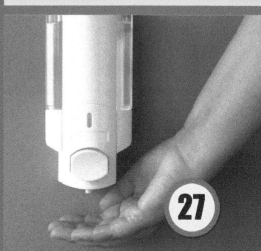

27

How to Wash Your Hands

To keep safe from COVID-19, you should wash your hands often. You may have touched something that others have touched. This could be a door handle, railing, or countertop. Never touch your eyes, nose, or mouth. This is how COVID-19 enters the body. Washing your hands for at least 20 seconds with soap can kill COVID-19.

1. Use soap.

2. Wash each palm.

3. Wash the backs of each hand.

(28)

4. Wash between each finger.

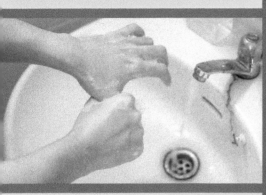

5. Wash the base of each thumb.

6. Wash fingernails in each palm.

7. Rinse hands.

8. Dry hands.

Quiz

Test your knowledge of COVID-19 by answering the following questions. The questions are based on what you have read in this book. The answers are listed on the bottom of the next page.

1 What is used to make a virus look bigger?

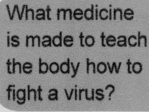

2 How many kinds of coronaviruses can survive in humans?

3 How far should people keep away from others?

4 What medicine is made to teach the body how to fight a virus?

5 What can be made with a 3D printer?

6 How long should people wash their hands with soap?

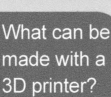

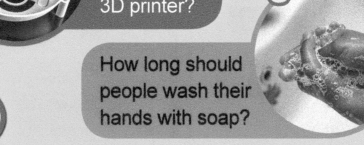

Explore other levels in the COVID-19 series.

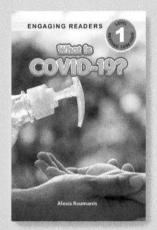  

Visit www.engagebooks.com to explore more Engaging Readers.

About the Author

Alexis Roumanis graduated from Simon Fraser University's Master in Publishing program in 2009. Since then, he has edited hundreds of children's books, and written more than 100 educational books. His audience includes children in grades K-12 as well as university students. Alexis lives with his wife and three young boys in British Columbia, Canada. He enjoys the outdoors, reading a good book, and has a passion for learning new things.

Answers:
1. A microscope 2. Seven 3. 6 feet (2 meters) 4. A vaccine 5. Breathing masks 6. At least 20 seconds